TEACH FOR SUCCESS

Successful Strategies for All Students Including Students with Special Needs

By

Karel DiFranco

1663 LIBERTY DRIVE, SUITE 200
BLOOMINGTON, INDIANA 47403
(800) 839-8640
WWW.AUTHORHOUSE.COM

First published by AuthorHouse 01/25/05

ISBN: 1-4208-0034-5 (sc)

Library of Congress Control Number: 2004097082

Printed in the United States of America
Bloomington, Indiana

This book is printed on acid-free paper.

DEDICATION

To my husband, Sam DiFranco
For his support and encouragement

And to All Teachers
Whose Passion is to Teach

About The Author

Karel DiFranco is a college instructor at Meredith College in Raleigh, North Carolina. Currently she teaches psychology courses, with a particular interest in "Exceptional Psychology," a course required by future teachers focusing on the interests and needs of individuals with disabilities in the educational setting.

She holds a Master's degree in Special Education from Buffalo State College, Buffalo, NY with dual certification in elementary (K-6) and special education (K-12), majoring in learning and behavioral disorders. She also has a Master's degree in School Administration and Supervision from Niagara University, Niagara University, NY. Her teaching experience totals 24 years, with diverse employment in regular and special education programs.

CONTENTS

Introduction: How to Use This Book

Nothing is more important than helping students succeed in the learning environment. As a teacher, you can maximize the potential for this success by increasing students' confidence little by little, day-by-day. As a result, you can foster the enthusiasm for learning. In every possible way, we need to motivate success and the desire for learning. Nothing is more exciting than educational experiences that promote the "I can do it," attitude. Providing students with the confidence to succeed is what teaching is all about.

Education is one of the most challenging professions today. For new teachers to develop into truly good teachers and experienced teachers to remain good teachers, they need to assume the responsibility of a life-long learner. This means there is a need to continually acquire new information through staff development and collaboration with other teachers on a regular basis. All new teachers should spend a portion of their day in the faculty room, sharing information, exchanging ideas, and learning about each other personally and professionally. It is important not to isolate yourself from the teaching faculty and environment. Regardless of how teachers are prepared, teachers will require continual professional development and training to optimize student performance that makes teaching more effective and rewarding.

I wrote this book as a resource for increasing your success as a teacher, thus, making the educational experience more satisfying and worthwhile. From my experiences with learning and behaviorally challenged students, my dedication for helping students succeed is a passion that will always be with me.

These practical, ready-to-use strategies and techniques have been proven successful in my own classroom experiences. In addition, effective strategies have been selected from a variety of my favorite educational resources.

This book can be read in a relatively very short time. It is intended to be a resource for identifying strategies that work. Make this a multisensory experience. Recite, take notes, highlight, underline, and utilize the notebook pages for your own personal note taking. Checkboxes are included with each strategy and you are encouraged to check the ones you find useful to put into action. Jot down your thoughts, feelings, and any information that is worthwhile. You will be amazed how helpful your notes can be for future educational assignments and experiences.

As you read this book, consider how you can work more efficiently with learning differences. Make a personal commitment to discover, explore, and experiment in a variety of ways. Use techniques, strategies, and behavior modifications that compliment learning. Effective techniques contribute to the continuous improvement of educational leadership, student success, as well as enhanced positive relationships with others around you. You will see a difference in your work with students, your co-educators, and ultimately, in your own personal success in the classroom.

Characteristics of Effective Teaching: *Practical Strategies and Techniques in the Classroom.*

Today more than ever, there is a population of students with diverse learning needs. No longer can a teacher teach to the group, one must teach to the individual. To ensure an effective educational environment for all students, individual learning differences need to be accounted for and instruction needs to be adapted to reach learners with varying levels of ability. This does not mean you have to change a total curriculum to accommodate all students, but simply implement a variety of proven strategies and techniques, such as those outlined in this book. The best news is that when you find strategies that work with students with learning difficulties, you may also observe that they are effective with other students as well. It does not only benefit students with learning differences, but all students. An important note to mention to new teachers, the first years of teaching are the most challenging. New teachers are sometimes assigned to the least desirable classrooms, are required to prepare multiple subjects, or assigned to the most challenging group of students. The learning environment you create, the adaptation of a flexible curriculum, and the behavioral methods you use to discipline will surely affect how successful your students will be in the classroom.

Effective teachers recognize and appreciate the differences among students and the willingness to accommodate all students with learning differences. This includes students with learning disabilities (LD), attention deficit hyperactive disorder (ADHD), attention deficit disorder (ADD), speech and language difficulties, and various social, emotional, and health impairments. Students with learning challenges have specific learning needs. They may require more help in areas such as reading comprehension, math calculations, essay writing, organization, or study skills. Some special education advocates recommend incorporating these services into the regular education curriculum as the way for providing beneficial educational programs. As a result, general education teachers are responsible for the education of all students. Special education and regular education programs are no longer isolated or separate programs. Effective programs establish collaborative partnerships to design optimal programs for including students with learning differences within the regular classroom. Successful partnerships are characterized by shared-decision making, shared planning, and co-teaching relationships. Teachers need continuous training in effective teaching strategies, curriculum adaptations, and behavior management programs to be truly effective in the educational environment. All teachers want to be competent and all students want to achieve success.

The integration between regular education and special education is very evident in education today. The inclusion of special education students within the regular class is a common practice. The focus of special education has shifted from an emphasis on what and how to teach to an emphasis on where to teach. Considerable evidence suggests that segregating special education students is actually detrimental to their academic and social development and those special students generally perform better in regular classrooms. Consequently, adaptations of instructional procedures for the regular classroom program may be necessary for special needs students, but many regular students might similarly benefit from these changes. As schools are challenged to effectively serve an increasingly diverse population of students, the concern is implementing inclusive education in ways for ensuring success for all students, especially those with special learning and/or behavioral needs.

Most students with mild to moderate disabilities and various learning differences can be successful in the general education program through collaborative efforts among teachers, special education faculty, support staff, and parents. This book aims to provide effective techniques and strategies for helping students with learning differences become more successful within the educational setting. It is important to note: Do not expect immediate improvement! Patience and persistence are essential. Changing or modifying inappropriate behavior is a task that requires time, effort, and commitment. Providing structure and consistency is key: communicating clear expectations, enforcing appropriate rules, and implementing reasonable consequences.

Fictitious names of students are provided to help describe characteristics of students who are challenged and struggle with the daily expectations and responsibilities of the academic environment. Each chapter will be organized by using a checklist and notebook paper is provided for your own ideas and personal information.

Strategies are provided in seven specific areas:

- **Structure and Organization**

- **Learning Styles**

- **Behavior Management**

- **Adaptive Curriculum**

- **Cooperative Learning**

- **Active Parent Involvement**

- **Positive Attitude Assures Positive Results**

Chapter One

Structure and Organization

Johnny is characterized as a student who does not possess good study habits, such as poor listening, inattention, and dependency on others to complete assignments. He wastes time, is easily distracted by other students, and talks too much in class. He rarely completes class work and homework assignments. It is apparent that Johnny has the potential to do average work, but tests grades are barely passing.

These behavior characteristics are commonly associated with the descriptions of LD and ADHD/ADD students. Other students are characterized as disorganized, forgetful, procrastinators, or inefficient planners. Sometimes students like Johnny do not have the ability to accomplish tasks independently. Consequently, teachers and parents often assist with the student's daily tasks and responsibilities. Establishing structure, routine, and consistent classroom procedures facilitates independence so that eventually – after some weeks or even months – students can be successful on their own. During this time, support systems are essential. Classroom organization includes a number of factors: physical arrangement of class space, routines for academic and nonacademic activities, classroom climate, accommodations for individual differences, and classroom management.

✓ **Effective techniques and strategies:**

☐ Post classroom rules as a visual reminder and review frequently.

☐ Write classroom rules so that they are specific, concise, positive, and clearly understood by students.

☐ At the beginning of each lesson, display an agenda explaining the objectives of the lesson. Consistently use written lesson objectives.

☐ Provide the student with a list of discussion questions for reading assignments. This will assist the student in focusing on important material.

☐ Establish routines for handing in work, heading papers, classroom entrance routine, etc.

☐ Organize the classroom so there is one location or procedure for handing in daily assignments.

☐ Post daily/weekly schedule in the same location.

☐ Post all of the assignments on a weekly homework board. Keep adding to the board and leave it up for the entire week. This will assist any student who has been absent from class.

☐ An assignment notebook should be utilized to record homework assignments and important dates.

☐ At the end of each day or class period, take five minutes and have students check their assignment notebooks to see what is necessary to take home. Many students are unsure of what is required for next day assignments.

☐ Expect all assignments to be recorded, and monitor that students have done so. Double-check students' assignment notebooks to make sure they are adequately up-to-date; initial your approval or comments. If necessary, assign student partners to check each other and initial each other's notebooks.

☐ Provide a calendar for students to record long-term assignments.

☐ Organize a project assignment into daily/weekly tasks.

☐ Color-code textbook covers, notebooks, and folders by academic subject. It is often helpful for students to have books and materials for the same subject in the same color. For example, math books and folders are blue; science is red, etc.

Students respond more favorably to an environment that is structured, orderly, and predictable. Creating structure in the classroom can also prevent discipline problems. Effective classroom managers do not wait until a problem occurs; instead, they anticipate potential problems prior to the occurrence. Take a problem prevention approach.

Structure and Organization

Establishing structure, routine, and consistent classroom procedures facilitate independence so that students can eventually be successful on their own.

Chapter Two

Learning Styles

David *has difficulty with listening in class. For example, he has a hard time following verbal directions, maintaining concentration, and taking notes during class lectures. He always seems to be two steps behind the other students. He is usually the last person to get his books and materials ready and has difficulty finding a specified page. When a verbal direction is given, he looks around to see what the other students are doing.*

Individuals learn through their senses, perceptions, and experiences. David has difficulty with auditory processing and struggles in the classroom when information is delivered verbally, especially during lectures and class discussions. Our senses provide the pathway for learning, and most students learn best through a particular sensory modality. In every class, there will be a combination of learning styles: visual learner, auditory learner, and tactile or kinesthetic learners. Effective teachers use a variety of techniques, methods, and activities to benefit all learning styles.

Learning styles are simply different approaches to, or ways of learning. Most of us tend to have strengths and preferences for learning when processing information through sensory modalities. (i.e. seeing, hearing, touching). Knowing strategies and techniques for various learning styles helps students learn more effectively, by offering them a chance to learn material using their preferred modality.

Types of learning styles:

Visual Learners. For most students, the strongest sensory modality is sight. These students learn by seeing and observing others. Visual learners need to see the instructor's body language and facial expressions to fully understand the content of the lesson. They learn best from visual displays including pictures, diagrams, charts, overhead transparencies, videos, handouts, and graphic organizers. During a lecture, visual learners often prefer to take detailed notes, in order to see the information for an optimal learning experience.

✓ **Visual learners benefit from:**

☐ Educational video tapes and television programs

☐ Charts, pictures, and posters while lecturing

☐ Computer software to supplement learning

☐ Observing rather than reading through live-action demonstrations (videos, models, and examples)

☐ Graphic organizers (mapping, story maps, charts, and outlines)

☐ Opportunities to write out words during spelling bees and games

☐ Overhead projector presentations, especially in conjunction with additional features, including color, underlining, and guided outlines

☐ Writing key words or phrases for students to copy during lectures or discussions

Auditory Learners. Auditory Learners receive information best through listening. They benefit most from verbal lectures, group discussions, and reciting information.

✓   **Auditory learners benefit from:**

☐ Oral readings of stories/textbook materials

☐ Participating in small and large group discussions

☐ Listening to stories and textbook materials on audiotapes

☐ Sound-enhanced computer programs

☐ Computer games for review, reinforcement, and rewards

☐ Recording notes on tape and review by listening

Tactile/Kinesthetic Learners. Tactile learners appreciate touching, moving, and doing. They learn best through a hands-on approach, actively exploring the physical world around them. These students benefit from the use of manipulatives in learning through their sense of touch. Kinesthetic learners do best when the information learned is tied to a motion. For example, tapping or clapping out sounds and/or syllables in words. These students need opportunities to participate in learning games, laboratory experiments, drawing and construction, and use of interactive computer programs.

✓   **Tactile-kinesthetic learners benefit from:**

☐ Hands-on activities while learning

☐ Manipulatives for math calculations whenever possible

☐ Computer word processing instead of handwriting

- ☐ Blank outlines for note-taking for lectures and textbook reading

- ☐ Highlighting important information while note-taking

- ☐ Game-like activities for review

- ☐ Using clay, sand, or sandpaper for learning vocabulary/ spelling words

- ☐ Dry-erase boards or individual chalkboards for practice and review

- ☐ For independent review, the following materials may be used for learning letters and words through tracing and writing exercises: finger paints, flannel board, pipe cleaners, or stencils.

- ☐ Reading must be an active process. Utilize the **SQ3R Method** for reading textbook material (Coon and Woodward, 1986). The letters S-Q-R-R-R stand for Survey, Question, Read, Recite, and Review. The five steps facilitate comprehension, increase memory of facts, and serve as a study guide for tests. By the way, I recommend this technique to all my college students who have difficult preparing for tests and organizing important textbook reading material.

   S = Survey. Survey the entire chapter. Skim over the pictures, captions, lesson objectives, vocabulary words, and chapter review.
   Q = Question. For each bold heading, identify one or more questions that the section is likely designed to answer.
   R = Read. While reading the chapter, answer each question developed from the previous Question step. Read each section and then create new questions as you progress through the chapter.
   R = Recite. Read questions and answers out loud.

R = Review. When you have finished reading, skim back over the chapter and review your notes. Review all learning and information.

Most LD students benefit from a multisensory approach. It is necessary to use every available channel for learning and retaining knowledge. This approach utilizes as many learning styles and modalities as possible. By appealing to multiple senses, students seem to better organize and integrate information in the brain more efficiently. In addition, the multisensory instructional approach should be combined with information repetition and review, so that students master the material.

Consciously, incorporate multiple learning modalities into your lesson planning and activities. Many teachers have a dominant teaching style. If you primarily favor one teaching style, student achievement decreases. If you use lecturing as your major teaching tool, this favors auditory learners – the least effective learning style among students. Utilize visuals regularly. Charts, diagrams, pictures, overheads, and brief portions of videos or films are highly recommended to compliment learning. Also, whenever possible, provide hands-on experiences. Using multiple modalities increases student understanding, interest, and motivation.

Learning Styles

In every class there will be a combination of learning styles: visual learner, auditory learner, and tactile-kinesthetic learners. Effective teachers use a variety of techniques, methods, and activities to benefit all learning styles.

Chapter Three

Behavior Management

Joe is the type of student labeled as a behavior problem. He is described as disruptive, aggressive, and uncooperative. He regularly defies authority, saying things like, "This class is stupid and boring." He attracts his peers' attention by saying inappropriate comments in class. His schoolwork is careless, messy, and incomplete. Generally, he appears to be a very unhappy and angry person.

Teachers often dislike and struggle with students like Joe. Instead of finding ways to encourage students, teachers become more discouraging and find ways to punish and exclude students. Teachers need to find more nurturing and supportive ways to assist Joe in the classroom. Successful teachers are effective behavior managers. One of the most important and challenging jobs of teaching is managing and correcting behavior. Effective behavior management techniques utilized in the classroom creates a positive environment for learning. Positive expectations are key to successful behavior management.

Students with behavior problems are the most difficult to manage. Low intrinsic motivation, repeated failure, teasing, name-calling, and peer rejection all adds up to "I don't like school and I don't want to be here." These examples of negative thoughts and negative self-talk develop into noncompliance, disrespect, and disruption in the classroom. This creates a situation that challenges all teachers.

An essential and important part of all educational programs is a behavior management system. The knowledge of operant learning principles for correcting behavior is very powerful. The basic principles of any effective behavior management program are the identification of desirable and undesirable behaviors as well as incorporating positive consequences for appropriate behavior and negative consequences for inappropriate behavior.

It is necessary to consistently implement consequences for both desirable and undesirable behavior. Providing rewards for desirable behavior and negative consequences for undesirable behavior teaches students the differences between acceptable and unacceptable behaviors in the classroom. Conscious awareness of behavioral principles is a basic, yet essential part of an effective classroom environment.

Basic principles of behavior management include:

- Structure, organization, and effective planning

- Positive rewards for appropriate behavior (i.e. adult attention, words of praise, token economy systems which include stars, stickers, points etc.)

- Negative consequences for inappropriate behaviors (i.e. time-out, loss of privileges, overcorrection, and response cost.)

✓ **Effective techniques and strategies:**

☐ Frequently provide positive reinforcements for desirable behaviors. Use a variety of reinforcers (compliments, words of praise, a pat on the back, a hand shake, free time, eliminate homework assignments, prizes etc.).

☐ Give immediate, positive, and corrective feedback.

☐ Use a behavior contract for specific behaviors you want to correct (homework completion, attendance, increasing on-task behaviors, improving test grades, decreasing talkative behavior etc.).

☐ Seat the distractible student near a nondistractible model (teacher or student).

☐ Seat the distractible student in front of classroom, close to instruction.

☐ Have students clear their desks of distractible items, allowing only essential materials on the desk.

☐ Provide a specific time-out area that is not reinforcing.

☐ Celebrate students' efforts and successes utilizing a bulletin board.

☐ Greet students everyday at the doorway with a smile.

☐ Clearly and consistently state behavior expectations and prepare to follow through with consequences for misbehavior.

☐ Reward students regularly. Rewarding positive behavior increases positive behavior. Positive incentives include:

- Positive notes or phone calls to parents
- Award certificates for excellent test grades
- Increased recess time
- Special class activity, party, movie at the end of the month
- Awarded a "no homework pass" for exceptional work or behavior
- Free tickets awarded for school activities, sports, or cafeteria items
- Tickets awarded for future prizes/raffles
- Play a game with other students/teacher
- Lunch with the teacher
- Ice cream party or pizza party

- Individual or class earned free time for listening to music, games, computer time, or activity of choice
- No homework on Friday
- Remember to praise small successes. It is better to put a +4 on the paper instead of a – 6.
- Sit by a friend for one period
- Be a teacher's helper.
- Excused from pop quiz
- Five minutes of talk time at the end of the period of class
- Free reading time
- Game activity day
- Movie with popcorn

When dealing with difficult-to-manage students, sometimes it is necessary to employ behavioral consequences that go beyond the classroom environment or the classroom time period. Positive relationship building between teacher and student is essential; a social component students with behavior problems rarely share with others. Students need to feel that teachers care about them.

In my experiences with difficult and struggling students, providing positive consequences or rewards for behavior outside the classroom is extremely beneficial for building sound relationships. In-class rewards, such as recess, privileges, and prizes were not enough to encourage the behavior I expected. Extending this reward system beyond the classroom might include activities such as kite flying, bowling, miniature golf, and ice cream and pizza gatherings. When activities like this were initiated, something amazing happened. The relationship dominated by authority changed. I was not only a teacher who managed, instructed, and disciplined, I also became a person who enjoyed many of the activities that students liked. A new relationship developed – a relationship dominated by shared interests, mutual caring, and fun. These outside class activities are recommended for small group rather than one-on-one activities.

When students realize that you do care about them and enjoy their company, a new relationship also develops in the classroom. As a result, students begin to respond more positively and appropriately in the classroom. This also gave me opportunities to increase communication and establish positive relationships with parents. When teachers, parents, and students develop positive relationships, the classroom experience then becomes more positive, effective, and successful.

As a first-year teacher, I was assigned to an intermediate, self-contained special education class composed of learning and behavior disabled students. I realized then, my role as a behavior specialist was just as important as my role of a curriculum specialist. I expected students to report to school willing to learn, but this expectation was not apparent in this classroom. The role as a behavior manager was the main focus of my attention and extremely necessary for a group of students. Common rewards such as good grades, words of praise, and special privileges were simply not reinforcing. Some students require concrete evidence in association with a desirable behavior. If necessary, some behavior management programs often utilize a **token economy system.** This system is characterized by students earning artificial rewards (i.e. points, stars, or tokens) for desirable behaviors. These tokens are then later exchanged for actual rewards when a specific goal is achieved.

Behavior impaired students are often characterized by anxiety and low self-esteem. This deflated confidence is often coupled with learning difficulties. Due to repeated failures and the daily frustrations of school expectations, students commonly demonstrate low intrinsic motivation, the internal motivation that assists carrying out academic responsibilities.

Their own personal internal system lacks energy and drive. As a result, the motivation to succeed in the educational environment is almost nonexistent. Due to this, the need to motivate externally assumes greater significance. Using token reinforcements can be very effective. The external rewards associated with successful experiences directly increase internal motivation. The belief that, "I feel good and I can do this!" increases the "I can be successful"

23

attitude. Anything that puts a smile on a student's face, such as a sticker for commendable behavior, is worthwhile.

✓   **Group or individual successes should be rewarded regularly:**

☐ Utilize the Goody Jar. Take a large transparent container and put it on the teacher's desk for all students to see. Whenever a student exhibits a desirable behavior, praise the student, and let him/her throw a handful of popcorn kernels into the jar. Look for desirable behaviors and reward regularly. When the jar is filled with kernels, reward the class with popcorn and a movie. This strategy rewards the individual, but it also contributes to a group-scale reward, thereby modeling for the student how individual actions can benefit others around them. That is, it shows students what they do has a positive impact beyond them and the rest of the class benefits, which can be a pretty powerful lesson.

☐ Roll of Tickets. Obtain a roll of raffle tickets and place it on your desk. When a student demonstrates an appropriate behavior, give the student a ticket. Have them write their name on the back of the ticket and put into a decorated container. Five winners are picked from the container after a designated period of five weeks, eight weeks, or at the end of each marking period. Students then receive prizes.

☐ Lucky Squares. Construct a bulletin board or get a large dry-erase board and draw one hundred, two-inch squares. When a student demonstrates a good behavior, he/she can pick a square and sign his/her name. When all squares are taken, the board is labeled. At the top of the board, the horizontal row of squares is labeled alphabetically, and the vertical row of squares is labeled numerically. When ready, place the letters in one container and the numbers in a separate container. Then pick one letter and one number to get a specific combination (i.e. B-5). Find the square that corresponds to B-5 to find the lucky winner. Repeat five times, for a total of five winners. Prizes are then awarded to the winners.

Another important component of behavior management is problem prevention. Most of us react to behaviors and provide consequences after inappropriate behaviors occur. If we can deal effectively with minor misbehaviors, this can eliminate more serious behaviors developing later. In my training with students with behavioral concerns, initially dealing effectively with minor misbehaviors is essential. It is also important to mention, not a single one of these techniques is new. These effective strategies are utilized and implemented in many special education classrooms. It is the conscious and planned awareness of such techniques that make them effective. In every way possible, it is easier to apply preventive techniques rather than wait for more difficult situations to emerge. You will find these simple, easy-to-use strategies useful in any classroom. The following techniques and strategies were addressed years ago in college textbooks (Redl and Wineman, 1957) and are still referred to as components of effective behavioral management programs today. (Friend and Bursak, 1999)

✓ **Problem Prevention Techniques:**

☐ Planned Ignoring. This is a simple technique that eliminates behavior simply by ignoring it. As long as a behavior is tolerable, for example, a student who snaps their fingers to answer a question, ignoring this behavior leads to faster elimination than interference. At this moment, it is more effective to call on the student who is appropriately raising his/her hand to answer the question. Reward students who are behaving appropriately. Again, focus on the positive, and ignore the negative.

☐ Signal Interference. This technique applies the power of nonverbal signals or gestures to ward off potential problem behaviors. Common signals are making direct eye contact, silently positioning yourself at the front of the room with your arm raised above your head, and flicking off the light switch. These are all ways in which teachers communicate to students to stop what they are doing and pay attention. Simple gestures can interfere or prevent the disruptive behavior before it starts or gets worse.

☐ Proximity Control. Moving closer to the student who exhibits the misbehavior(s) can easily eliminate inappropriate behavior(s). This can effectively be implemented without interrupting instruction. During a lecture or activity, simply rotate around the room. Do not stay in one location.

☐ Involvement in Interest Relationship. Take an interest in the student who appears to be losing interest or who may be off-task. The student who seems to be disinterested and anxious will regain interest when the teacher just asks a few questions about what he/she is doing and provides individual attention and interest in the task he/she is performing.

☐ Tension Reduction Through Humor. Use humor to deflate potentially disruptive behaviors. In some situations, a humorous reaction may actually make it possible for the student to get relief from the "laughter" of the moment. As a result, it curbs the behavior. A teacher can respond to a student who sleeps in class, "Looks like sleeping beauty needs her beauty rest." In this case, humor works like a diversion and counteracts the misbehavior.

☐ <u>Hurdle Help</u>. When students run into an obstacle that prevents completing a task successfully, some unwanted outbursts, due to frustration and anxiety, can be demonstrated. For example, a student who is taking a test, getting frustrated by the moment, may slam the desk and tear up his/her paper. Therefore, producing a discipline concern for the teacher. Some students just need a little help to get over the hurdle. By assisting with directions, or asking leading questions to facilitate comprehension, this can prevent negative reactions.

☐ <u>Removing Distracting Objects</u>. It is not unusual for students to bring toys, gadgets, candy, or distractible items that interfere with instruction. Before beginning instruction, remind students to put such items away. If objects are a continuous distraction, teachers should usually hold them for "safe-keeping." It is important to return items promptly at the end of the class period or class day. Asking the student to help remind you before leaving the classroom is a good idea. You can bet that students will not forget personal possessions.

☐ <u>Restructuring</u>. No matter how thorough you are with lesson planning, for some unknown reason, some of the best-made plans go wrong. For some students, listening to a story can be unstimulating or the challenge of learning a difficult concept can be overwhelming. Unexpected problem behavior can surface. Restructuring means stopping the present ineffective activity and move to another plan or activity. Temporarily, provide a break or have a backup plan. When students are becoming restless and inattentive, instead of reprimanding or punishing, simply take care of the misbehavior in a proactive way. Allow students to get up and stretch, or provide a five-minute break to eliminate some of the negative energies. Always be prepared with an alternative plan.

Preventive behavior management methods are essential as well as reactionary methods that include application of consequences for unwanted behaviors. Eliminating undesirable behaviors through punishment (providing negative consequences) is another principle in behavior management. Although, positive reinforcement is a proactive strategy more powerful than punishment, providing negative consequences for inappropriate behavior can also be effective.

Providing Negative Consequences

It is important to stress that providing negative consequences, not simply as a way to punish or demonstrate hostility, can be an efficient way to teach students the need and expectation to behave appropriately in the classroom. Be aware, punishment can be reinforcing to students especially if they are only receiving attention for inappropriate behaviors. Since negative attention can be reinforcing for some students, inappropriate behaviors will increase. It is not uncommon for students characterized with behavior disorders to misinterpret punishment with intentional ways to humiliate, show feelings of dislike, display rejection and so forth. Frequent scolding, reprimanding, and punishment send the message to students, "I don't like you and I don't care about you." These feelings can create more difficult classroom conditions. For those students, the application of punishment techniques is especially ineffective because it only reinforces the dysfunctional system in which they already operate. Be mindful that students who regularly warrant negative consequences are probably that way because they receive more than their share of negative consequences outside of the classroom. In addition, if the student receives added peer attention from acting out in class, negative consequences may be unproductive to compete with the strong desire for peer attention. Therefore, dispensing negative consequences can actually encourage the student to repeat the same behavior in the future. To mention again, teachers are more successful when they consciously use positive rather than negative strategies. For this reason, only a minimal portion of this book will address Punishment Techniques: Loss of privileges, overcorrection, time-out, and response cost will be discussed.

✓ **Punishment Techniques:**

☐ Loss of privileges

- Loss of recess or free time
- Teacher calls or conferences with parents
- Student writes an essay or brief summary explaining the cause of the inappropriate behavior and identifying alternative ways of handling similar situations in the future. Do not use a repetitive statement (i.e. I will behave in class, 100 times.) as a corrective measure. It is more effective to have a student write something more meaningful that requires thinking and a certain level of difficulty.
- Student writes an apology note.

☐ Overcorrection is associated with correcting the behavior so that it is restored back to its original state, an unpleasant task.

    When a student breaks a rule, for example, writes on his/her desk, the student spends time after school or during recess cleaning all the desks in the classroom.

☐ Time-out involves removing a misbehaving student from opportunities for rewards. This technique is associated with the removal of positive reinforcement. It refers to some type of isolation or separation of the student from the classroom when an unacceptable behavior is demonstrated.

Time-out can be used in various ways. In one approach, students are able to observe other students but cannot interact with them. Students who misbehave can sit away from classroom activities and not participate. For example, a student is sent back briefly to his/her desk for not cooperating in a group activity. In the next approach, students can also be excluded from observation of classroom activities. A student can be seated well away from class activity, in the corner of the room facing the wall or in a location designated for this purpose. (i.e. study carrel) Lastly, for older students and more disruptive behaviors, students are excluded in separate rooms. This is usually another room located away from the classroom providing an undesirable environment with a few desks and chairs supervised by another adult. This type of time-out involves a preplanned location with another teacher or administrator and a school-wide discipline policy.

Adapted from Friend and Bursuck (1999), the following considerations are extremely important when using time-out:

1. ***The length of time-out should be brief but effective.*** It should vary depending on the student's age, the violation, and the time it takes to decrease the demonstration of undesirable behaviors. Depending on the age of the student, the time spent away from reinforcement should last five to ten minutes. It is very important that students not be separated from the rest of the class for long periods of time.

2. ***Do not pay attention to the student while in a time-out session.*** Remember, attention can be misinterpreted as reinforcing. While the student is in time-out, no coaching or verbal explanations should take place at this time.

3. ***Time-out should be associated with a location that is highly visible and supervised.*** Placing a student in the hallway can be very reinforcing, especially for those students who are looking for a way out of classroom

assignments and responsibilities. Being excused from schoolwork, talking to students who are passing in the hallways, and freedom to roam can be extremely rewarding. If you use it frequently, students will miss important amounts of instruction time. A good guideline to remember, if any punishment technique is used frequently, this indicates that the consequence is somewhat rewarding and ineffective. If you find yourself repeating the same consequence very often, then switch to another one. Be consciously aware of this. In addition, it is important to assign another time period set aside for missed instruction during time-out. For example, the student should be required to make-up this time before or after school instruction.

4. *If a student refuses to go to a time-out location, you may need to escort the individual or ask for assistance.* If time-out becomes a power struggle between student and teacher, then it might not be worth pursuing. Remember, what works for one student may not be appropriate for another student. It is important to have a toolbox of strategies available.

✓ **Response Cost** involves the removal or loss of something the student values or desires. It is a system that takes away points, privileges or some other reward when an inappropriate behavior occurs. (i.e. for inappropriate comments, hitting, swearing, etc.) Many response cost programs utilize a token economy system.

☐ Establish a system of tokens. Tokens can be used to track behavior on a daily basis. Basically, students are given a set number of tokens at the beginning of each day. For example, this can be a group of popsicle sticks for young students and points or circles drawn on a 3X5 inch index card for older students. Each time a student demonstrates an unacceptable behavior, a token is taken away. If the student has any remaining at the end of the session or day, the agreed upon reinforcement is delivered.

☐ <u>One-minute wait after class</u>. According to Lee Canter (1992), this is a simple and effective technique. The student is denied the privilege of being dismissed. Simply, the student waits one minute after dismissal for lunch, recess, or the next period class. During the one-minute wait, take the opportunity to discuss the circumstances surrounding the misbehavior, and the consequences that will follow.

☐ <u>Class-wide Approach</u>. Write the word RECESS, or the name of a specific privilege on the board. Each time an inappropriate behavior is demonstrated, one of the letters is eliminated or taken away. If any letters remain, students are rewarded with a special privilege. If no letters remain, the privilege is denied.

Response cost programs can be used with individuals or total class management systems to reduce inappropriate behaviors in the classroom.

When utilizing any response cost program, positive reinforcement strategies, implemented simultaneously, are essential and should not be ignored in your total management program. Again, I do want to emphasize that token economy systems are most effective when used primarily to reward positive behavior.

Since many students with special needs have deficits in learning coupled with poor social interaction skills, they may experience frequent frustration due to academic deficiencies and inadequacies in peer relationships. As a result, behavior problems may occur more frequently than not. When addressing the subject of student behavior, problem prevention is just as critical as problem resolution. Regularly reinforcing appropriate behaviors encourages students to behave responsibly and reduces problem behaviors.

Always Focus on the Positive. The most important thing to remember is to reinforce and reward desirable behavior. It is the most powerful, effective recognition you can give. Most teachers and parents have a tendency to reinforce undesirable behaviors and ignore desirable behaviors, thereby causing desirable behaviors to decrease and undesirable behaviors to increase. This tendency is usually unconscious and not obvious to most teachers. Always focus on the positive; positively reinforce appropriate behaviors regularly. The more positive you become as a teacher, role model, and leader, the more positive the people and the environment becomes around you. Let students know that you notice their efforts.

Behavior Management

Effective behavior management techniques utilized in the classroom creates a positive environment for learning. Positive expectations are key to successful behavior management. Conscious awareness of behavioral principles is a basic, yet essential part of an effective classroom environment.

_____

_____

_____

_____

_____

_____

_____

_____

_____

_____

_____

_____

Chapter Four

Adaptive Curriculum

***Lisa** has difficulty with getting her thoughts down on paper and completing most writing assignments. She frequently uses sentence fragments with little attention to grammar, punctuation, and capitalization. In addition to poor sentence structure, her manuscript is sloppy, immature, large, and unevenly spaced. Cursive writing is a very difficult, frustrating task that takes additional time for Lisa to complete.*

Lisa has a language learning disability in the area of expressive language. She struggles with expressing her ideas in writing. Teachers need to find alternative ways for her to be successful. All children can learn and be successful, although not on the same day, in the same time, or in the same manner. Learning is a continual process of adaptation for some students to meet the expectations and demands of school. These students do not learn as quickly or as efficiently as other students and are constantly experiencing stresses against time and failure. They must somehow learn to deal with a system that allows little change for learning and behavioral differences. However, students with learning problems can often be successful when accommodations are provided in the classroom. Success can only be achieved when educators remain open-minded, flexible, and demonstrate the willingness to constantly adjust to meet the needs of students.

Teachers must be adaptable, provide extra support during instructions, and modify assessment techniques to ensure success from all students. Accommodations consist of changes in the method in which children are taught, including changes in instruction, completing assignments and homework, and testing. Adaptive instruction requires learning as well as applying various strategies that will facilitate the ability to meet the expectations of the learning environment. It seeks to enhance student performance in a given subject by modifying the way in which instruction is delivered and by changing the environment where the learning takes place. An adaptive curriculum uses a variety of instructional procedures, materials, as well as testing modifications to help students master the requirements of the curriculum.

✓ **Provide modifications for completion of assignments:**

☐ Minimize lengthy copying activities or provide the information on worksheets or handouts.

☐ Encourage students to practice typing skills or use the word processor to complete homework assignments.

☐ Fold or divide math paper into sections. Place one problem per box.

☐ For students with more severe visual-perceptual problems, use graph paper for calculating 2- and 3-digit numbers. Writing each numeral in a separate box to keep the numbers organized and aligned properly for calculation is recommended.

☐ Allow extra time to complete assignments.

☐ Always check for understanding before the students begin the assignment. Check by asking questions and confirm responses.

☐ To ensure comprehension, have students demonstrate their understanding by working out the first example.

☐ Allow the use of tools and aids, such as multiplication charts and tables, spell check devices, calculators, etc.

☐ For textbook assignments, provide cloze procedure activities to check comprehension. For example, Abraham Lincoln was the ____ president of U.S.

☐ Have students repeat directions out loud for the rest of the class. This will benefit students with processing deficits as well as others who are initially not listening.

☐ Break long-term assignments into manageable chunks so that work can be accomplished as independently as possible. Modify the length of the assignment. If the assignment is long, assign each section and allow the student to complete one section at a time over a period of days, each accompanied by reasonable due dates.

☐ Modify the classroom-spelling list by shortening the number of words on the list.

☐ Assign optional projects whenever possible. This allows students to be creative and work in ways that are most suited to their abilities.

✓ **Utilize techniques during classroom lectures and activities:**

☐ Provide a simple outline of the class lecture, which can be used as a guide for taking notes and preparing for tests.

☐ When asking a question, allow extra time for students to process information. Do not assume students are not knowledgeable and unprepared. Provide clues and hints.

☐ Provide mnemonic strategies for retaining information. Utilize the first letter technique or silly sentence. (i.e.

"King plays chess on fiber glass stools." – kingdom, phylum, class, family, genus, species)

☐ Provide more time for practice and review. Increase the amount of practice and review in a variety of formats. (small groups, peer-tutoring, teacher-directed, game formats etc.)

☐ Repeat relevant words/features during lectures and note-taking activities.

☐ For students who have difficulty copying notes, supply notes with key blank spaces that the student can fill in during the lecture presentation or provide a blank outline with main topics and subtopics.

☐ Introduce a lesson by identifying its main points. Copy and leave plenty of room between each heading for student notes. Optionally, direct students to supply five facts under each main heading. This collection of notes gives students with weak auditory memory and organizational skills something to both organize their thinking and help them remember better.

☐ To ensure student comprehension of material covered, break lectures into 15 or 20-minute segments. Follow each segment with 3-5 review questions.

☐ Utilize strategies that allow you to individualize instruction. This includes grouping, peer tutoring, independent work, learning centers and teacher-made materials.

☐ Repeat major points frequently. Slow down speech, pause more, and repeat as needed.

☐ Frequently review and reinforce previously taught skills. Use weekly quizzes.

☐ For notes on the board, emphasize important details by underlining, circling, or marking with a star or check mark.

☐ Present questions for class discussion both orally and visually by writing them on the board, overhead projector, or written handout.

☐ For students who have weak reading skills, tape essential parts of the textbook; make use of films, charts, and pictures.

☐ End each lesson with practice and a review. Before going on to new material, go back and review the previous information. Repetition is an important part of learning.

✓ **Provide accommodations for test preparation and test taking:**

☐ To reduce test anxiety, provide students with sample test questions. Also, knowing what to study may increase the motivation to study more.

☐ Teach strategies and skills for taking a variety of tests.

☐ Develop periodic reviews for the entire class before giving a test.

☐ Avoid handwritten tests, especially in cursive.

☐ Provide a study guide for tests. A few days in advance is highly recommended, 3-5 days.

☐ Enlarge, underline, or highlight key words on test items.

☐ Provide test modifications for students as appropriate. For example, allow extra time, a special location with minimal distractions, or modified test formats.

Some students will require accommodations and special adaptations to the physical environment, the curriculum, the way instruction is provided, and assignment requirements. Whenever possible, specialized conditions should be designed to benefit not only students with special needs, but also all students so they can participate more fully and successfully in classroom activities.

Adaptive Curriculum

An adaptive curriculum uses a variety of instructional procedures, materials, as well as testing modifications to help students master the requirements of the curriculum.

_____

_____

_____

_____

_____

_____

_____

_____

_____

_____

_____

_____

Chapter Five

Cooperative Learning

Mary *is considered a low-achiever. She requires continuous assistance with initiating and completing assignments. She demonstrates low self-confidence and rarely volunteers in class discussions. She does not raise her hand if she needs assistance, leaving the assignment unfinished. Socially, Mary is a loner and is very quiet. She plays alone on the playground and rarely interacts with other students.*

Mary is the type of student that would benefit from interacting with her peers. She would benefit from classroom activities that encourage group learning and peer assistance. Advocates of cooperative learning believe that students can learn from each other, benefit from each other's strengths, and develop teamwork skills. Facilitating small group learning means helping group members understand the importance of working together, sharing ideas, and interacting in helpful ways. Cooperative learning refers to classroom procedures in which students work on learning activities in small groups and receive grades or recognition based on the group's performance. It encourages all students, of varying levels of ability, to interact with each other in a positive setting.

Teachers use cooperative learning activities because they want to see all students actively talking, working, and interacting. Students are assigned to groups on the basis of their ability. Generally, a group is composed of high-achieving, average, and low-achieving students. Group projects enable students to combine their knowledge and skills to complete an assignment. The task is assigned to the whole group and the goal is to create a finished product based on the collaboration of contributions from the group members.

Be careful! It is important to closely supervise and structure activities to ensure all students participate. Some students will try to take over the group, telling other students what to do, and then do all the work themselves. This is not the purpose of this technique. It is painful to see students being excluded by the group. Initially, it is important to provide structure and assign specific tasks to each member in the group. This guarantees active participation from each member. At the same time, the teacher should closely and positively reinforce individual students for their contribution to the group task. Public recognition, (i.e. words of praise), is a key intervention for successful group learning. If the teacher publicly praises a low-achieving student, competencies are likely to result in increased activity as well as self-confidence and motivation to participate, both now and in the future. The teacher's job is a manager; monitor the groups by walking around and briefly observing each. This should not be used as a time to supervise from afar, or sitting at your desk and catching up on paper work. The teacher's role is to monitor the groups and to praise students when cooperative behavior is demonstrated.

✓ **Cooperative learning methods:**

☐ Peer tutoring benefits students who need direct instruction and extra assistance with regular class responsibilities and assignments. Possible activities include organizing materials, checking accuracy of recording homework assignments, drill and practice, and test review and preparation.

Slavin (1980) describes a variety of cooperative learning techniques in which students work on learning activities in small groups and receive grades or rewards based on the group's performance. The jigsaw method and student teams-achievement divisions are two of his commonly known techniques.

☐ **Jigsaw.** The jigsaw approach assigns students to heterogeneous teams ensuring different ability levels. The teacher organizes teams in advance. Learning material is divided into sections according to the number of team members. Each member of the cooperative learning group will be responsible for a specific part of the project and each student is responsible for studying or preparing their assigned potion. Students are responsible for studying his/her portion with other teammates who have the same task from another group. After students have thoroughly studied, they return to their original team to teach it to their group. Lastly, each team member is quizzed on all aspects of the unit. The approach is beneficial for studying science and social studies information or any textbook reading material. This technique can be modified for preparing group projects (i.e. book reports, biographies, and research projects). For example, a report involving the biography of a famous American, each group member is assigned to research and write about a different part of the American's life. To assure individual accountability, grading the group members individually, rather than as a whole, might be necessary.

☐ **Student teams-achievement divisions.** Four to five students are assigned to heterogeneous learning groups. The teacher introduces the material to be learned and then provides study work sheets to team members. Students complete and study the material with their team members until everyone understands the material. Next, students take a 15-minute quiz individually. The quiz scores are used to compute a team score. In modification, the scores can be recorded as individual grades.

Corners and Graffiti are additional techniques adapted from Kelly (1997).

☐ **Corners.** Corners is a cooperative learning activity that enables students to choose and discuss a particular topic or subject. For this activity, students can work in pairs or small groups. To facilitate the activity, different topics are posted in designated corners of the room. Each student selects a specific corner based on information received from the teacher. For example, names of important story characters are posted in each corner. The teacher has the students choose a character in the book that they would like to report about and respond to the following questions located in that corner. The following day, students are assigned to another corner and the activity is repeated.

☐ **Graffiti.** Graffiti is a technique that facilitates brainstorming and can be especially effective as a prewriting activity. Give each group colored markers and a piece of paper that can cover a large area so all group members can write at the same time. Each group member is given a different colored marker so it is easy to identify each individual's contribution. Groups are given a different question or topic, which requires answers using words, phrases or graphics. For example, "Favorite holiday activities," "Write down your ideas of what a perfect world would be like," or "What current event in the news concerns you the most?" The activity continues until each group returns to their original topic. Then, each group reads all new comments. With this additional information each group can discuss, summarize, or possibly present this information to the class.

Cooperative learning activities can be an effective learning experience involving contributions of different ability levels to complete a task. Facilitating small group learning means helping group members appreciate the importance of working together and interacting in helpful ways. Of course, the methods shared in this chapter can be simplified and modified for almost any type of academic activity. The methods have been provided as a guideline to encourage your own creativity to involve students learning together rather than independently.

Cooperative Learning

Cooperative learning activities can be an effective learning experience involving contributions of different ability levels to complete a task. Facilitating small group learning means helping group members appreciate the importance of working together and interacting in helpful ways.

_____

_____

_____

_____

_____

_____

_____

_____

_____

_____

_____

_____

_____

_____

_____

○ _____

_____

_____

_____

_____

_____

○ _____

_____

_____

_____

_____

○ _____

_____

_____

ACTIVE PARENT INVOLVEMENT

It is well acknowledged that a key element for a successful school experience is parent involvement, an essential part of a quality school program. Successful students have supportive parents who take an active part in their child's school responsibilities, activities, and experiences. When parents are involved and play a supportive role in their child's education, children do better in school. Building positive partnerships with parents result in positive benefits to students' education and aim toward strengthening the home-school relationship. It is important for teachers to provide suggestions, listen attentively, and communicate regularly with parents. Here are a few suggestions for partnering with parents.

✓ **Parent Involvement Strategies:**

☐ At the beginning of the year, send parents an introductory letter. In the letter, provide your name, subject, phone number, and email address. A positive first communication is important for parents to feel more comfortable to contact a teacher if a problem or concern is necessary for discussion.

☐ Send home "happy notes." This can be done on an individual basis, (i.e. to praise a specific behavior or recognize test grades) or as a monthly newsletter to recognize student achievements.

☐ Make personal phone calls to parents to recognize students' achievements and efforts.

☐ Ask parents to look at the papers and materials that their children bring home. Recommend that they comment on the work and look over the mistakes with their children. When a parent shows a genuine interest in their child's work, it communicates the idea that education is an important priority and encourages students to do well in school.

☐ Talk to parents about establishing effective study habits at home. Parents should provide a quiet, nondistractible study area. Do homework in a place free of distractions, with the TV, stereo, and computer off. Set up a desk, table, or area designated for study, not far away from parent supervision.

☐ Students work best when a parent is present even if assistance is not provided. Parents should assist their children with keeping to task, preventing off-task behavior. It is important for parents to assist, but not complete assignments for the student.

☐ Give the student the opportunity to choose the study time, although it should be daily and consistent. It is recommended to have a consistent study time so a routine can be established. If no homework is assigned, this time should be spent reviewing material or independent reading.

☐ Encourage parents to read with their children. Reading for fun and discussing the material helps develop the child's interest in reading.

☐ For reading homework assignments, encourage reading as partners. Parents can take turns reading each paragraph or page with their child. Review main ideas and vocabulary.

☐ Communicate homework procedures. Some teachers have students maintain an assignment notebook to record daily assignments. If there is no assignment, students are required to write "no homework" following that specific subject. Parents should review assignment notebooks daily and can be asked to check and sign the book. This extra supervision keeps parents informed of assignments and provides opportunities for communication between parent and teacher.

☐ Recommend to parents that they use a monthly calendar to record long-term assignments that is highly visible to all family members.

☐ Ask parents to check all homework to see that it is completed and put directly into a notebook, a homework folder, and book bag, so that it is ready to be taken to school the next day.

☐ Encourage parents to take an active part and interest in their children's school work, by providing regular reminders, assisting with reviewing daily work, helping organize book bags, and preparing for tests.

☐ Encourage parents to verbally praise children when homework is completed and for all successful school experiences.

☐ Encourage parents to reward successful school experiences. Rewards don't have to be expensive to be effective. Best rewards involve time, not money. Examples include:
  • Special one-on-one time with parent
  • Skipping a chore

- Having a friend over for dinner
- Extra play time or free time
- Getting to stay up late
- Choosing a favorite meal
- Ice cream treat
- A bicycle ride together
- Going to the movies

☐ Invite parents into the classroom as guest readers or speakers, student assistants, special activity coordinators, etc.

Active parent involvement directly correlates to increased student success. Developing partnerships with parents, reporting regularly to parents, and encouraging the expertise of parents in classroom activities are just a few ways for increasing parent-family participation. All this is linked to a common cause – helping students succeed. Establishing good working relationships with parents and families improves the school experience for students. Most educators recognize the importance of parental involvement in the schooling of children and this can be especially crucial for students with special needs. Teachers, parents, and students should gain a cooperative relationship to ensure success in both the school and home learning environments.

Active Parent Involvement

Successful students have supportive parents who take an active part in their child's school responsibilities, activities, and experiences. Children do better in school when parents are involved and play a supportive role in their child's education.

_____

_____

_____

_____

_____

_____

_____

_____

_____

_____

_____

Chapter Seven

Positive Attitude Assures Positive Results

Teachers face numerous challenges in the classroom, making the job seem overwhelming at times. There will be many days that trigger the feelings of incompetence. For example, you might think, "I didn't connect with my students," or "I didn't manage behavior effectively," and "I didn't communicate clearly with parents." When your class seems to be out-of-control, making you feel powerless, you tend to perceive these experiences pessimistically. This type of thinking leads to increased frustration, stress, and negativity.

Be proactive. Learn from it. Instead, look at these events as learning experiences. Ask yourself, "*What can I learn from this, so that it won't happen again?*" Personal reflections and attitudes determine how we perceive and respond to the daily events and challenges. When you perceive yourself as ineffective, you are more likely to feel lethargic, unhappy, and unmotivated. Maintaining a positive self-image helps keep you motivated, energetic, and enthusiastic.

To help foster this positive attitude, there are two simple questions that you can ask yourself at the end of each day?

1. What went well today that I should continue?
2. What did not go well today that I should change?

Take the time to record daily successes. It is important to realize how significant a list of effective strategies or successes can help increase your self-confidence, making you more effective in the classroom. Focus on the positive aspects of the classroom. This will help you cope with whatever challenges come your way.

✓ **Five Simple Daily Reminders to Maintain a Positive Attitude:**

☐ Today, smile while teaching. It is contagious. It is amazing how many students will smile back at you.

☐ Today, greet students at the door with a positive compliment. (i.e. "Wow, you look nice today," or "I see you have your homework, great!") Simply, set a goal of using a number of positive phrases each day so that positive thoughts can become a part of your daily routine.

☐ Today, check for your students' comprehension of material covered in class. According to S. Winnebrenner (1996), this simple strategy is known as the "Ticket Out the Door." Create a brief form or ticket for students to respond to the following two questions:
  ▪ What did I learn (understand) today?
  ▪ What did I not understand today?

  Pass these "tickets" out at the end of the class period, and then refer to them to develop or adjust lesson plans accordingly.

☐ Today, look for ways to increase student success. Utilize a variety of positive reinforcements, token economies, and special privileges.

☐ Today, appreciate the joy of this day. Always, look on the bright side. A good attitude promotes a positive outlook.

Successful teachers provide a positive and structured learning environment, one that accommodates learning differences. It is a warm, nurturing, and friendly environment that welcomes all students. The important message to communicate regularly to students: **I like you. I care about you and I want you to be successful**. This begins with the teacher being an effective leader, manager, and a teacher who is a good role model. Model the behaviors you want in your classroom. If you want to have more cooperative and responsible students, be a more understanding and cooperative teacher. Successful teachers are sensitive and open-minded. They are understanding of diverse learning needs and demonstrate a friendly, proactive attitude. Effective teachers create a trusting and caring environment where students have a sense of what they do matters and their sense of accomplishment is rewarded. Thus, successful teachers recognize the countless possibilities for enhancing positive growth and development. They show a personal interest in students as individuals, and this has a positive influence on their learning.

Based on my experiences with teaching regular and special needs students, and from my observations of successful educators, I truly believe that the information brought to you in this book will improve your effectiveness as a classroom teacher. Have fun rewarding desirable behaviors! Use the techniques that compliment your personality and teaching style(s), but also remember to use a variety of styles and techniques in order to motivate all learners. It is all up to you to recognize and develop them. In the end, these strategies will help increase student productivity, parent cooperation, and teacher effectiveness. Let your successes and your students' successes be your reward. **Celebrate the success for all — Teach For Success.**

Positive Attitude Assures Positive Results

Take the time to record daily successes. Focusing on the positive aspects of the classroom will help you cope with whatever challenges come your way.

_____

_____

_____

_____

_____

_____

_____

_____

_____

_____

_____

References

Association for Supervision and Curriculum Development. (Oct. 2003). Teaching all students. *Educational Leadership*, Vol.61, No.2.

Association for Supervision and Curriculum Development (Nov. 2001) Understanding learning differences. *Educational Leadership* , Vol.59, No.3.

Association for Supervision and Curriculum Development (Feb. 1996) Students with special needs. *Educational Leadership*. Vol.53, No.5.

Canter, Lee and Canter, Marlene. (1992) *Assertive discipline: positive behavior management for today's classroom*. Santa Monica, CA: Lee Canter and Associates

Children and Adults with Attention-Deficit/Hyperactivity Disorder (CHADD) (2000) *The CHADD information and resource guide to ADHD*. Landover, Maryland: CHADD.

Coon, Dennis and Woodward, Carole (1986) *Introduction to psychology: exploration and application*. St. Paul, MN: West Publishing Co.

Friend, Marilyn and Bursuck, William (1999) *Including students with special needs: A practical guide for classroom teachers*. Needhan Heights, MA: Allyn and Bacon Publishing.

Hardman, Michael; Drew, Clifford and Egan, M.Winston.(2002) *Human exceptionality: society, school, and family*. Boston MA: Allyn and Bacon Publishers.

Kelly, Pat (1997) *Preparing students with disabilities for higher learning and performance based assessment.* Professional development seminar presented by Orleans/Niagara BOCES. March 1997, Lockport, NY.

Lavoie, Richard D. (1990) *How difficult can this be? The F.A.T. City Workshop.* (Videocassette) Available from PBS VIDEO, 1320 Braddock Place, Alexandria, VA 22314. Phone: 1-800-344-3337.

Redl, Fritz and Wineman, David. (1957) *The aggressive child.* New York, NY: The Free Press, A Division of MacMillan Publishing Co., Inc.

Reif, Sandra F. and Heimburge, Julie A. (1996) *How to teach and reach all students in the inclusive classroom: ready to use strategies, lessons and activities for teaching students with diverse learning needs.* West Nyack, NY: Center For Applied Research in Education.

Slavin, Robert E. (1980). Cooperative learning. *Review of Educational Research,* Summer, 1980, Vol.50, No.2, pp.315-342.

Winebrenner, Susan (1996). *Teaching kids with learning difficulties in the regular classroom: strategies and techniques every teacher can use to challenge and motivate struggling students.* Minneapolis, MN: Free Spirit Publishing, Inc.

Winkler, Henry and Oliver, Lin. (2003) *Hank Zipper, The most true confessions of the world's best under achiever. Niagara Falls or Does it?* New York, NY: Grosset and Dunlap Publishing.

For additional information, speaking engagements or hosting a seminar in your area, contact:

Karel DiFranco
919-676-5912
difrancok@hotmail.com

www.ingramcontent.com/pod-product-compliance
Lightning Source LLC
Chambersburg PA
CBHW030413290526
45785CB00004B/1990